National 5
Mathematics
Practice Papers for SQA Exams

Mike Smith

Contents

HODDER
GIBSON
AN HACHETTE UK COMPANY

The Publishers would like to thank the following for permission to reproduce copyright material:

Acknowledgements: Exam rubrics at the start of each paper copyright © Scottish Qualifications Authority.

Every effort has been made to trace all copyright holders, but if any have been inadvertently overlooked the Publishers will be pleased to make the necessary arrangements at the first opportunity.

Although every effort has been made to ensure that website addresses are correct at time of going to press, Hodder Gibson cannot be held responsible for the content of any website mentioned in this book. It is sometimes possible to find a relocated web page by typing in the address of the home page for a website in the URL window of your browser.

Hachette UK's policy is to use papers that are natural, renewable and recyclable products and made from wood grown in sustainable forests. The logging and manufacturing processes are expected to conform to the environmental regulations of the country of origin.

Orders: please contact Bookpoint Ltd, 130 Park Drive, Milton Park, Abingdon, Oxon OX14 4SE. Telephone: (44) 01235 827720. Fax: (44) 01235 400454. Lines are open 9.00–5.00, Monday to Saturday, with a 24-hour message answering service. Visit our website at www.hoddereducation.co.uk. Hodder Gibson can be contacted direct on: Tel: 0141 848 1609; Fax: 0141 889 6315; email: hoddergibson@hodder.co.uk.

© Mike Smith 2016
First published in 2016 by
Hodder Gibson, an imprint of Hodder Education,
An Hachette UK Company
211 St Vincent Street
Glasgow G2 5QY

Impression number   5 4 3 2 1
Year   2020 2019 2018 2017 2016

Cover photo copyright © jlpfeifer/123RF.com.
Illustrations by Aptara, Inc.
Typeset in Din Regular 12/14.4 pt. by Aptara, Inc.
Printed and bound by CPI Group (UK) Ltd, Croydon, CR0 4YY

A catalogue record for this title is available from the British Library

ISBN: 978 1 4718 8160 2

Introduction

National 5 Mathematics

Welcome to this set of Practice Papers, designed to give you experience in the types of questions, the format of question papers, and how to set out your solutions to gain full marks!

The solutions also link you to *How to Pass* so you can use the two books to revise and prepare effectively for the National 5 mathematics exam.

Know your course

The course comprises three Units:

- Expressions and Formulae (EF)
- Relationships (R)
- Applications (A)

The table below gives you an overview of the topics/course content within each Unit. The 'operational skills' refers to your 'toolbox' of skills, while 'reasoning skills' is how you use your 'toolbox' to solve problems and communicate solutions.

Expressions and Formulae	Relationships	Applications
Operational skills		
Algebraic skills ■ Expanding brackets ■ Factorising expressions ■ Completing the square ■ Algebraic fractions	**Algebraic skills** ■ Equation of straight line ■ Linear equations and inequations ■ Simultaneous equations ■ Change the subject of a formula ■ Quadratic functions: graphs ■ Quadratic equations	
Geometric skills ■ Gradient ■ Arc and sector of a circle ■ Volume (includes rounding to significant figures)	**Geometric skills** ■ Theorem of Pythagoras ■ Properties of shapes ■ Similarity	**Geometric skills** ■ Vectors
	Trigonometric skills ■ Trigonometric functions: graphs ■ Trigonometric relationships	**Trigonometric skills** ■ Area of triangle ■ Sine/cosine rules ■ Bearings

Expressions and Formulae	Relationships	Applications
Operational skills		
Numerical skills ■ Surds ■ Indices		**Numerical skills** ■ Percentages ■ Fractions
		Statistical skills ■ Interquartile range ■ Standard deviation ■ Scattergraphs and ■ Line of best fit
Reasoning skills		
■ **Interpret** a situation where mathematics can be used and **identify a strategy** ■ **Explain or justify** a solution and/or **relate it to the context** of the question		

Know your exam

To gain a course award, you must pass all three Units and the Course Assessment (the examination set by SQA). This exam will test skills beyond the minimum competence required for Unit Assessments.

The course is graded A to D, the grade being determined by the total mark you achieve in the final exam. Your exam is structured as follows:

Paper 1 (Non-calculator)	1 hour	40 marks
Paper 2 (Calculator allowed)	1 hour 30 minutes	50 marks
Totals	2 hours 30 minutes	90 marks

Know how to prepare

Mathematics should be regarded as a VERB; that is, it is a DOING WORD! **Doing** mathematics questions is the best use of your study time – practice makes perfect! You will benefit a lot more from doing questions than reading notes or copying from a textbook.

When DOING questions, practise showing **ALL YOUR WORKING**. Instructions in the exam papers clearly state that 'Full credit will only be given where the solution contains appropriate working'.

Attempt every question, and every part of every question! Even if you cannot do one part of a question, you may still be able to do another part – so do not give up!

Do not leave blanks – write something down as all working has to be checked and there may be a line worth a mark or two! Never score out working unless you have replaced it with something better.

A method that some use while answering questions is the 'CUBE' method.

C	Circle the COMMAND word(s)
	Write down, State, Calculate, Determine, Show that, Will the ...
U	Underline the KEYWORD(s) or phrases
	Increase in value, standard deviation, system of equations, parabola ...
B	Box the NUMBERS
	Put a box round any numbers given to highlight: increase of 5%, $3\cdot2 \times 10^4$ ...
E	Explain your ANSWER
	For example, if it is a volume question, don't just say $x = 40$, write volume $= 40\,\text{cm}^3$, that is, give context.

This method is particularly useful in some of the wordier questions, as it trains your eye to focus on and highlight the important parts, while pushing the other stuff to the back. Here is an example:

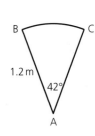

A spiral staircase is being designed. Each step is made from a sector of a circle as shown.

The radius is 1·2 m.

Angle BAC is 42°.

For the staircase to pass safety regulations, the arc BC must be at least 0·9 metres.

Will the staircase pass safety regulations?   4 Marks

So, using CUBE you might do the following:

A spiral staircase is being designed. Each step is made from a <u>sector of a circle</u> as shown.

The radius is 1·2 m.

Angle BAC is 42°.

For the staircase to pass safety regulations, the <u>arc BC</u> must be at least 0·9 metres.

Will the staircase pass safety regulations?   4 Marks

This will let you see that it is an arc/sector type question – so your mind focuses on that. 'Will the' indicates a reasoning type question, and the numbers are clearly highlighted in boxes.

Your solution would look like this:

$$\text{Arc} = \frac{\text{angle}}{360}\,\pi d$$

$$= \frac{42}{360}\,\pi \times 2.4 \ (r = 1\cdot2\,\text{m so } d = 2 \times 1\cdot2 = 2\cdot4)$$

$$= 0\cdot879\,\text{metres}$$

The staircase **does not** pass safety regulations as $0\cdot879 < 0\cdot9$ (**E**xplain your answer).

The next table shows how the course content is spread across the papers – so you can choose to focus on a particular topic or do a part or complete paper.

Good luck in your National 5 Mathematics exam!

Revision grid

	Knowledge Assessment Standards	Practice Paper					
		A1	A2	B1	B2	C1	C2
Expressions and Formulae (EF)	1.1 Applying numerical skills to simplify surds/expressions using the laws of indices	Q5 Q9	Q2	Q3 Q4 Q5	Q1	Q5 Q7	
	1.2 Applying algebraic skills to manipulate expressions	Q2 Q4 Q7 Q14		Q2 Q6		Q3 Q8a Q10 Q12b	Q2
	1.3 Applying algebraic skills to algebraic fractions	Q10		Q9		Q12a	
	1.4 Applying geometric skills linked to the use of formulae		Q6 Q11	Q7	Q3 Q7 Q14		Q8
Relationships (R)	1.1 Applying algebraic skills to linear equations	Q3 Q11		Q8 Q12 Q13	Q2	Q2 Q9	Q4 Q6a
	1.2 Applying algebraic skills to graphs of quadratic functions	Q8	Q4	Q8 Q11		Q8a	
	1.3 Applying algebraic skills to quadratic equations	Q6 Q13			Q5	Q4 Q8b	
	1.4 Applying geometric skills to lengths, angles and similarity		Q12		Q9		Q3 Q9
	1.5 Applying trigonometric skills to graphs and identities		Q10		Q4 Q10	Q11	Q5 Q10
Applications (A)	1.1 Applying trigonometric skills to triangles which do not have a right angle		Q5 Q9 Q13	Q10	Q8 Q13		Q7 Q12
	1.2 Applying geometric skills to vectors	Q5 Q12	Q3		Q11	Q6	
	1.3 Applying numerical skills to fractions and percentages	Q1	Q1 Q7	Q1	Q12	Q1	Q1
	1.4 Applying statistical skills to analysing data		Q8		Q6		Q6b Q11

National 5 Mathematics

HODDER
GIBSON
AN HACHETTE UK COMPANY

Paper 1 (non-calculator)

> **Total marks: 40**
>
> Attempt ALL questions.
>
> **You may NOT use a calculator.**
>
> Full credit will be given only to solutions which contain appropriate working.
>
> State the units for your answer where appropriate.
>
> Write your answers clearly in the spaces provided in this booklet. Additional space for answers is provided at the end of this booklet. If you use this space you must clearly identify the question number you are attempting.
>
> Use **blue** or **black** ink.
>
> Before leaving the examination room you must give this booklet to the Invigilator; if you do not, you may lose all the marks for this paper.

MARKS

1 Evaluate $2\frac{1}{4} \div \frac{5}{6}$.

2

[Turn over

2 Expand and simplify

$$(3x - 2)(x^2 - 3x + 1).$$

3

3 Solve the inequality

$$3 - x > 2(x + 3).$$

2

4 Factorise fully

$$3k^2 - 12.$$

2

5 Two forces acting on an object are represented by vectors **a** and **b**.

$$\mathbf{a} = \begin{pmatrix} 2 \\ -1 \\ -1 \end{pmatrix} \quad \mathbf{b} = \begin{pmatrix} 6 \\ 3 \\ -1 \end{pmatrix}$$

Calculate $|\mathbf{a} + \mathbf{b}|$, the magnitude of the resultant force.

Express your answer as a surd in its simplest form.

3

6 Prove that the roots of the equation $2x^2 + 5x - 3 = 0$ are real and rational.

3

7 Write $x^2 + 6x - 5$ in the form $(x + p)^2 + q$.

2

[Turn over

8 The diagram shows part of the graph of $y = x^2 - 6x - 7$.

A is the point $(-1, 0)$ and B is the point $(7, 0)$.

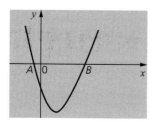

a) State the equation of the axis of symmetry of the graph.

2

b) Hence, or otherwise, find the minimum value of $y = x^2 - 6x - 7$.

2

9 Evaluate $8^{\frac{4}{3}}$.

2

10 Simplify $\dfrac{2}{k} + \dfrac{3}{k+2}$.

3

11 Mr Barclay bought four adult and two child tickets for a ghost tour.

The total cost was £76.

a) Using a for adult ticket and c for child ticket, write an equation to represent this.

Mrs Mackay bought three adult tickets and three child tickets for the ghost tour.

The total cost was £69.

b) Write another equation to represent this.

c) Calculate the cost of a ticket for an adult and the cost of a ticket for a child.

12 The diagram shows a tiling of congruent triangles.

Vector **u** is represented by $\overrightarrow{AB}$ and vector **v** is represented by $\overrightarrow{AF}$.

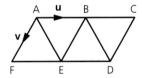

a) Express $\overrightarrow{AD}$ in terms of **u** and **v**.

b) Express $\overrightarrow{DB}$ in terms of **u** and **v**.

[Turn over

A

13 Solve the equation

$$2x^2 + 7x - 15 = 0.$$

3

14 Change the subject of the formula $a = b + 2c^2$ to c.

3

[END OF PAPER]

Paper 2

MARKS

1   The number of bees in a colony is increasing by 8% per week.

   There were originally 1800 bees in the colony.

   How many bees will be in the colony after three weeks?   3

[Turn over

2   The Earth is approximately $9 \cdot 3 \times 10^7$ miles from the Sun.

If 1 mile is equivalent to $1 \cdot 6$ kilometres, convert the distance from the Earth to the Sun from miles to kilometres.

Give your answer in scientific notation.

2

3 A is the point $(1, 3, 2)$.

$\overrightarrow{AB}$ is $\begin{pmatrix} 4 \\ 1 \\ -3 \end{pmatrix}$.

Write down the co-ordinates of B.

2

4   The diagram shows part of the graph of

$$y = (x + a)^2 + b.$$

Write down the values of a and b.

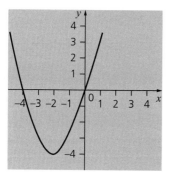

National 5 Mathematics

5 In triangle KLM, KL = 10 centimetres, angle MKL = 100° and angle KML = 30°.

Calculate the length of LM.

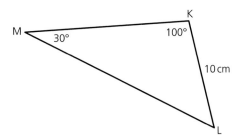

[Turn over

6 A glass paperweight is made in the shape of a hemisphere with a cone on top, as shown in the diagram.

The glass paperweight is 6 centimetres wide and 10 centimetres high.

Calculate the volume of the glass paperweight.

Give your answer correct to 2 significant figures.

5

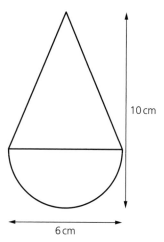

10 cm

6 cm

7 A car I bought last year depreciated in value by 15%.

It is now worth £12 500.

What was it worth when I bought it?

Give your answer to the nearest £100.

4

[Turn over

8 Brian looked at the price of a packet of pasta in six local shops.

The costs, in pence, were

52 48 57 46 54 49

a) Calculate the mean and standard deviation for this data.

3

Brian checked prices of the packets of pasta at local supermarkets and found that the mean price was 49 pence and the standard deviation 2·7 pence.

b) Make two valid comparisons between the two sets of data.

2

9 Window panes are in the shape of a rhombus.

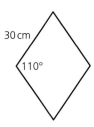

The side of each rhombus is 30 centimetres long.

The obtuse angle is 110° as shown.

Find the area of one window pane.

4

10 The diagram shows part of the graph of

$$y = a \sin x + b.$$

The line $y = 3$ is also shown.

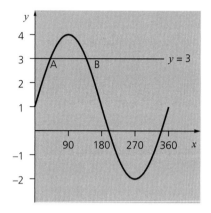

a) Explain how you can tell that $a = 3$ and $b = 1$.

2

b) Calculate the x-co-ordinate of the points A and B, where the line $y = 3$ cuts the graph.

4

11 The landing area for a discus in a discus-throwing competition is as shown.

The diameter of the circle is 2·5 metres.

The angle at the centre is 35°.

The length of each 'arm' is 25 metres from the centre of the circle.

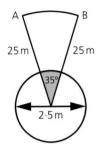

a) What is the area of the shaded sector in the circle?

3

b) What is the length of the outer arc AB?

3

[Turn over

A

12 A wooden frame has measurements as shown.

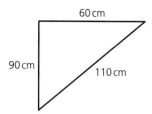

Is the frame in the shape of a right-angled triangle?

Show your working to justify your answer.

3

13 A lifeboat, L, picks up a distress call from a fishing boat, F, 42 kilometres away on a bearing of 110°.

At the same time another call from a sailing boat, S, comes in.

The sailing boat is at a distance of 16 kilometres on a bearing of 230° from F.

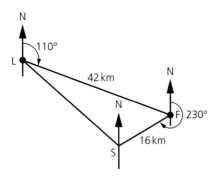

a) Calculate the size of angle LFS.

2

b) Hence calculate the distance from the lifeboat to the sailing boat.

3

[END OF PAPER]

National 5 Mathematics

HODDER
GIBSON
AN HACHETTE UK COMPANY

Paper 1 (non-calculator)

MARKS

1 Evaluate $1\frac{2}{3} + \frac{4}{7}$.   2

[Turn over

2 Factorise fully

$$25a^2 - 9b^2.$$

2

3 Evaluate $125^{\frac{2}{3}}$.

2

4 Multiply out the brackets and simplify

$$m^{\frac{1}{2}}(m^{\frac{1}{2}} - m^{-\frac{1}{2}}).$$

2

5 A right-angled triangle has dimensions as shown.

Calculate the length of AB, giving your answer as a surd in its simplest form.

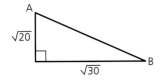

6 Change the subject of the formula $k = \sqrt{\frac{a}{b}}$ to a.

7 The area of a circle is $\frac{16}{\pi}$ cm².

Show that the circumference of the circle is 8 centimetres.

[Turn over

B

8 Given $f(x) = 5 - x^2$, evaluate $f(-3)$.

9 Express as a single fraction $\dfrac{1}{x} + \dfrac{2}{x-1}$.

10 In triangle ABC, AB = 6 cm and sin A = 0·75.

The area of triangle ABC = 18 cm².

Calculate the length of AC.

11 The Umbrella Company use a parabola for its 'U' logo.

The equation of the parabola is $y = (x - 3)^2 - 4$.

Part of the graph is shown in the diagram.

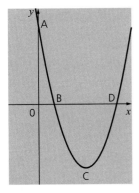

a) State the co-ordinates of the turning point C.

b) State the co-ordinates of point A, where the graph cuts the y-axis.

c) Calculate the length of the line BD.

[Turn over

MARKS

12 The graph below shows two straight lines.

$$y = 2x - 3$$
$$x + 2y = 14$$

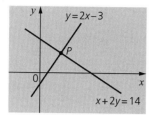

The lines intersect at point P.

Find, **algebraically**, the co-ordinates of P.

4

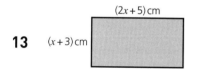

13 (x + 3) cm

a) Write down an expression, in terms of x, for the perimeter of the rectangle.

1

b) The perimeter of the rectangle is equal to the perimeter of the square.

Form an equation and find the value of x.

2

c) By how much is the area of the square greater than the area of the rectangle?

1

[END OF PAPER]

Paper 2

Total marks: 50

Attempt ALL questions.

You may use a calculator.

Full credit will be given only to solutions which contain appropriate working.

State the units for your answer where appropriate.

Write your answers clearly in the spaces provided in this booklet. Additional space for answers is provided at the end of this booklet. If you use this space you must clearly identify the question number you are attempting.

Use **blue** or **black** ink.

Before leaving the examination room you must give this booklet to the Invigilator; if you do not, you may lose all the marks for this paper.

MARKS

1   A light year, the distance light travels in one year, is approximately $5 \cdot 88 \times 10^{12}$ miles.

There are approximately $3 \cdot 15 \times 10^7$ seconds in one year.

How far does light travel in one second?

Give your answer in scientific notation, correct to 3 significant figures.   3

[Turn over

MARKS

3

2   Find the equation of the line shown in the diagram.

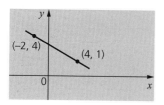

3 A fan is in the shape of a sector of a circle, as shown.

The radius is 14 centimetres.

The angle at the centre is 130°.

Calculate the perimeter of the fan.

4

 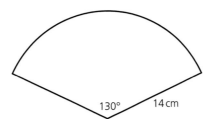

130°   14 cm

B

4 Show that

$$\frac{\sin^2 x}{(1 - \sin^2 x)} = \tan^2 x.$$

MARKS

2

34 National 5 Mathematics

5   Solve the equation

$$2x^2 - 3x - 7 = 0.$$

Give your answer correct to 2 significant figures.

[Turn over

6   A group of students sat a maths test.

Their marks, out of 50, were

14   23   42   12   46   13   48   32   33   47

a)   Calculate the median and the semi-interquartile range of these marks.

3

b)   A second group of students had a median mark of 28 and a semi-interquartile range of 21 marks.

Make two valid comparisons of the marks scored by the two groups of students.

2

7 A glass ornament is in the shape of a cone partly filled with water.

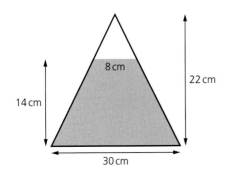

The cone is 22 centimetres high and has a base diameter of 30 centimetres.
The coloured water is 14 centimetres deep and measures 8 centimetres across the top.

What is the volume of water? **Give your answer correct to 2 significant figures**.

[Turn over

B

8   A triangle has dimensions as shown.

Calculate the size of angle x.

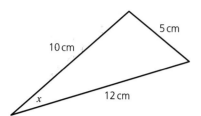

3

9 Two rectangular solar panels, A and B, are mathematically similar.

Panel A has a diagonal of 90 centimetres and an area of 4,020 square centimetres.

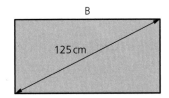

A salesman claims that panel B, with a diagonal of 125 centimetres, will be double the area of panel A. Is this claim justified? **Show all your working**.

4

B

10 Solve the equation

$$3 \sin x + 2 = 0 \quad 0 \le x \le 360.$$

3

11 The diagram shows vectors **u** and **v**.

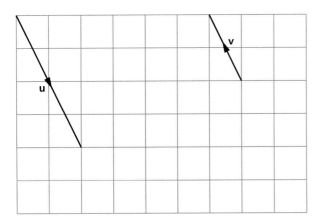

Find the components of **u** + **v**.

2

[Turn over

12 A computer cost £360 after VAT at 20% had been added.

What was the cost of the computer before VAT was added?

3

13 Hillwalker B is 400 m due East of hillwalker A.

The two hillwalkers take the bearing of a tree from each of their positions, as shown.

From hillwalker A the tree is on a bearing of 045°.

From hillwalker B the tree is on a bearing of 305°.

How far is it to the tree from the nearest hillwalker?

5

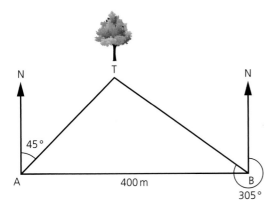

14 A cylindrical water tank, of diameter 120 centimetres, is partly filled with water.

The depth of the water is 25 centimetres.

What is the width of water, AB?

4

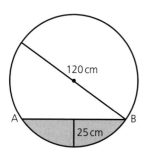

[END OF PAPER]

National 5 Mathematics

National 5 Mathematics

HODDER
GIBSON
AN HACHETTE UK COMPANY

Paper 1 (non-calculator)

MARKS

1   Evaluate $\frac{3}{4}$ of $3\frac{1}{2} - 1\frac{5}{8}$.   3

[Turn over

C

2 A line passes through the points A(1, –t) and B(3, 5t) as shown.

Find the gradient of the line, in terms of t.

2

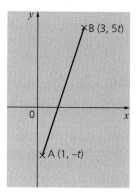

3 Multiply out the brackets and collect like terms

$$(3x + 4)(x^2 - 2x + 5).$$

3

4 Solve the equation

$$2x^2 - 5x - 3 = 0.$$

3

MARKS

5 Express $\sqrt{125} - 4\sqrt{5}$ as a surd in its simplest form.

2

6 ABCDEF is a regular hexagon, with centre G as shown in the diagram.

$\overrightarrow{AB}$ represents the vector **p**.

$\overrightarrow{CD}$ represents the vector **q**.

Find $\overrightarrow{BD}$ in terms of **p** and **q**.

2

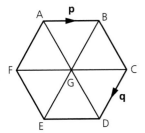

7 Multiply out the brackets and simplify

$$x^{\frac{2}{5}}(x^{-2} + 5x^{-\frac{2}{5}}).$$

2

[Turn over

8 a) $x^2 - 2x - 15$ is expressed in the form $(x + a)(x + b)$.

Find the values of a and b if $a > b$.

b) Hence, or otherwise, write down the roots of the equation
$$x^2 - 2x - 15 = 0.$$

c) The graph of $y = x^2 - 2x - 15$ is shown in the diagram.

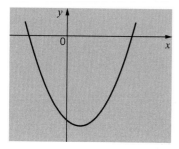

Find the co-ordinates of the turning point.

9 A test has twenty questions worth 100 points in total.

It consists of True/False questions worth 3 points each and multiple choice questions worth 11 points each.

How many multiple choice questions and how many True/False questions are in the test?

6

10 The formula for the volume of a sphere, radius r, is

$$V = \frac{4}{3}\pi r^3.$$

Change the subject of this formula to r.

11 In the right-angled triangle shown, BC, the hypotenuse, is 2 units in length.

Side AC is $2\sin x$ units in length.

Show that side AB is $2\cos x$ units in length.

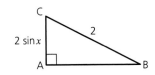

C

12 a) Simplify $\dfrac{b^2 + 2b}{5b + 10}$.

3

b) Factorise fully $6xy^2 - 15x^3y$.

2

[END OF PAPER]

Paper 2

Total marks: 50

Attempt ALL questions.

You may use a calculator.

Full credit will be given only to solutions which contain appropriate working.

State the units for your answer where appropriate.

Write your answers clearly in the spaces provided in this booklet. Additional space for answers is provided at the end of this booklet. If you use this space you must clearly identify the question number you are attempting.

Use **blue** or **black** ink.

Before leaving the examination room you must give this booklet to the Invigilator; if you do not, you may lose all the marks for this paper.

MARKS

1 After receiving a 3% pay rise, Patricia now earns £16 995.

   What did she earn before the pay rise?

   3

[Turn over

C

2 Express $x^2 + 2x - 1$ in the form $(x + p)^2 + q$.

MARKS

3 In the diagram, O is the centre of the circle and TR is the tangent to the circle at T.

Calculate x.

3

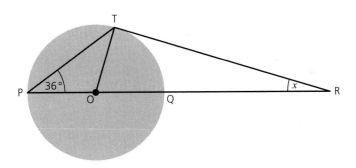

[Turn over

MARKS

4   The graph of the function $f(x) = 2x + 3$ passes through the points $(-4, b)$ and $(a, 11)$.

Determine the values of a and b.   3

5 Part of the graph of $y = a\cos x + b$ is shown below.

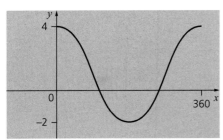

a) Explain how you can tell from the graph that $a = 3$ and $b = 1$.

b) Calculate the x-co-ordinates of where the graph cuts the x-axis.

[Turn over

C

6 The scatter graph shows the relationship between the age, A years, and value, V (£000s), of some cars in a showroom.

A line of best fit has been drawn.

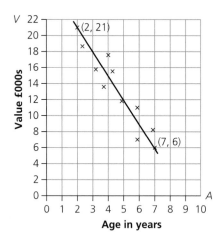

a) Find the equation of the line of best fit in terms of V and A.

4

b) Use the equation of the line of best fit to estimate the value of a car which is eight years old.

1

7 An aeroplane flies from its base, B, on a bearing of 040° for 300 kilometres.

It then changes direction and flies on a bearing of 150° for a further 550 kilometres.

The plane then returns directly to its base.

Calculate the distance of the last leg of the plane's journey back to its base.

4

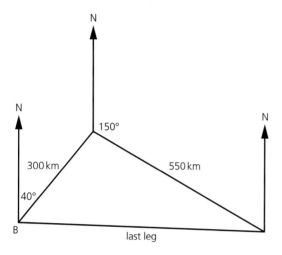

8 This conical glass can hold 125 millilitres of liquid when full.

The cone part is 10 centimetres tall.

Calculate the diameter of the glass.

4

10 cm

9 Calculate the length of AC.

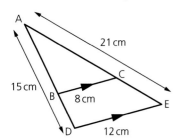

3

[Turn over

MARKS

10 a) Solve algebraically the equation

$$2 \sin x - 1 = 0 \qquad 0 \le x \le 360.$$

3

b) Hence, or otherwise, solve the equation

$$2 \sin \tfrac{1}{3} x - 1 = 0 \qquad 0 \le x \le 360.$$

2

11 The weight, in kilograms, of seven 6th Year students is as shown.

42, 58, 53, 62, 48, 51, 71

a) Calculate the mean weight for this sample.

b) Calculate the standard deviation for this sample.

The mean weight of all the 6th Year students was 62 kg.

The standard deviation was 8·2 kg.

c) Make two valid statements comparing the group of seven students with the whole year group.

[Turn over

C

12 The diagram shows a tower.

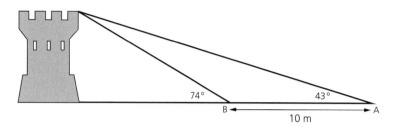

74°   43°   B ← 10 m → A

At A the angle of elevation to the top of the tower is 43°.

At B the angle of elevation to the top of the tower is 74°.

The distance AB is 10 metres.

Calculate the height of the tower.

6

[END OF PAPER]

National 5 Mathematics

HODDER GIBSON
AN HACHETTE UK COMPANY

Practice paper A

Paper 1 (non-calculator)

Question	Working	Mark		Note	Hint	HTP
1	$\dfrac{9}{4} \times \dfrac{6}{5}$ $= \dfrac{54}{20}$ $= \dfrac{27}{10}$	✔ ✔	2	Write mixed number as improper fraction. Solution (does not simplify further).	To divide, invert fraction and multiply.	See Chapter 1
2	$(3x - 2)(x^2 - 3x + 1)$ $= 3x(x^2 - 3x + 1) - 2(x^2 - 3x + 1)$ $= 3x^3 - 9x^2 + 3x - 2x^2 + 6x - 2$ $= 3x^3 - 11x^2 + 9x - 2$	✔ ✔ ✔	3	Split first bracket. Multiply out brackets. Collect like terms.	Cannot use FOIL as there are three terms in second bracket.	See Chapter 2
3	$3 - x > 2(x + 3)$ $3 - x > 2x + 6$ $-3 > 3x$ $-1 > x$ $x < -1$	✔ ✔	2	Multiply out bracket. Simplify. Write in 'correct way'.		See Chapter 5
4	$3k^2 - 12$ $= 3(k^2 - 4)$ $= 3(k^2 - 2^2)$ $= 3(k - 2)(k + 2)$	✔ ✔	2	Take out common factor. Identify difference of two squares. Factorise fully.	When factorising check: ■ common factor ■ difference of two squares ■ trinomial / quadratic.	See Chapter 2
5	$\mathbf{a} + \mathbf{b} = \begin{pmatrix} 8 \\ 2 \\ -2 \end{pmatrix}$ $\lvert \mathbf{a} + \mathbf{b} \rvert^2 = 64 + 4 + 4$ $= 72$ $\lvert \mathbf{a} + \mathbf{b} \rvert = \sqrt{72}$ $= 6\sqrt{2}$	✔ ✔ ✔	3	Use Pythagoras in 3D to find $\lvert \mathbf{a} + \mathbf{b} \rvert^2$. Take the square root to find the magnitude. Simplify the surd.		See Chapter 15

Question	Working	Mark		Note	Hint	HTP
6	$b^2 - 4ac$ $= 5^2 - 4(2)(-3)$ $= 49$ $49 > 0$ AND perfect square Therefore two real, distinct and rational roots	✔ ✔✔	3	Use the discriminant. Correctly substitute a, b, c. Interpret result.	Reminder: ■ $b^2 - 4ac = 0$: equal roots ■ $b^2 - 4ac > 0$: two real distinct roots ■ $b^2 - 4ac < 0$: no real roots	See Chapter 9
7	$x^2 + 6x - 5$ $(x + 3)^2 - 5 - 9$ $(x + 3)^2 - 14$	 ✔ ✔	2	$\frac{1}{2}$ of x co-efficient. Complete solution.		See Chapter 2
8 a) b)	$x = 3$ $y = 3^2 - 6(3) - 7$ $= -16$	✔✔ ✔ ✔	4	Find mid-point of AB and $x =$. Substitute into formula. Evaluate.	Axis of symmetry is mid-point of line joining zeroes.	See Chapter 8
9	$\sqrt[3]{8^4}$ $= 2^4$ $= 16$	 ✔ ✔	2	Rewrite with roots and powers.	It is usually easier to calculate the root first.	See Chapter 3
10	$\dfrac{2}{k} + \dfrac{3}{k+2}$ $= \dfrac{2(k+2) + 3k}{k(k+2)}$ $= \dfrac{5k+4}{k(k+2)}$	 ✔ ✔ ✔	 3	State common denominator. Correct numerator. Simplify.	Typical algebraic fraction-type question. 'Cross multiply' to get denominator and numerator.	See Chapter 4
11 a) b) c)	$4a + 2c = 76$ $3a + 3c = 69$ $12a + 6c = 228$ $6a + 6c = 138$ $6a = 90$ $a = 15$ $b = 8$ Adult ticket is £15. Child ticket is £8.	✔ ✔ ✔ ✔ ✔ ✔	6	Form equation. Form second equation. Set up simultaneous equations (e.g. eqn 1 × 3 and eqn 2 × 2). Find value of one variable. Find value of second variable. Ensure question is answered (i.e. do not just leave values of a and b).	This is typical wording for a simultaneous equations question. Check if question asks for values of variables – or for another calculation.	See Chapter 7

Question	Working	Mark		Note	Hint	HTP
12 a)	$\overrightarrow{AD} = \overrightarrow{AB} + \overrightarrow{BE} + \overrightarrow{ED}$ $= \mathbf{u} + \mathbf{v} + \mathbf{u}$ $= 2\mathbf{u} + \mathbf{v}$	✔		Find path. State in terms of $\mathbf{u}$ and $\mathbf{v}$.	2D vectors question. Find the path by looking for lines parallel to given vectors.	See Chapter 15
b)	$\overrightarrow{DB} = \overrightarrow{DE} + \overrightarrow{EB}$ $= \mathbf{u} - \mathbf{v}$	✔	2	(Other paths could be used.)		
13	$(2x - 3)(x + 5) = 0$ $x = \dfrac{3}{2}$ or $x = -5$	✔✔ ✔	3	1 mark for each bracket. 1 mark for solutions.		See Chapter 9
14	$a = b + 2c^2$ $a - b = 2c^2$ $\dfrac{a - b}{2} = c^2$ $\sqrt{\dfrac{a - b}{2}} = c$	✔ ✔ ✔	3	1 mark for subtracting b, 1 mark for dividing by 2. 1 mark for square root.	In a changing the subject question, do one step at a time.	See Chapter 5

Paper 2

Question	Working	Mark		Note	Hint	HTP
1	$1800 \times 1\cdot08^3$ $= 2267$	✔ ✔ ✔	 3	Use multiplier of 1·08. Power of 3. State answer.	100% + 8% 108% = 1·08	See Chapter 1
2	$1\cdot6 \times 9\cdot3 \times 10^7$ $= 14\cdot88 \times 10^7$ $= 1\cdot488 \times 10^8$	 ✔ ✔	 2	 Multiply. Rewrite in proper format.		See Chapter 3
3	$\begin{pmatrix} 1 \\ 3 \\ 2 \end{pmatrix} + \begin{pmatrix} 4 \\ 1 \\ -3 \end{pmatrix} = \begin{pmatrix} 5 \\ 4 \\ -1 \end{pmatrix}$ B $(5, 4, -1)$	✔ ✔	 2	Use vector. State in co-ordinate form.	Remember that a vector describes a movement.	See Chapter 15
4	$a = 2$ $b = -4$	✔ ✔	 2	Graph moved 2 left (halfway between −4 and 0 is −2). Graph moved 4 down.		See Chapter 8
5	$\dfrac{LM}{\sin 100} = \dfrac{10}{\sin 30}$ $LM = \dfrac{10\sin 100}{\sin 30}$ $= 19\cdot7$ cm	✔ ✔ ✔	 3	Use sine rule. Re-arrange. Calculate solution.	This is typical wording for a sine or cosine rule question.	See Chapter 16
6	$V = \dfrac{1}{2}\left(\dfrac{4}{3}\pi r^3\right) + \dfrac{1}{3}\pi r^2 h$ $= \dfrac{2}{3}\pi(3^3) + \dfrac{1}{3}\pi(3^2)(7)$ $= 108\cdot3$ cm³ $= 110$ cm³ (2 s.f.)	✔ ✔ ✔ ✔ ✔	 5	Use formulae for volumes of hemisphere + cone. Substitute values, including correct radius (half of 6 cm = 3 cm). Calculate (unrounded). Round correctly.	Compound volumes or 'conservation of volume' is a popular topic.	See Chapter 14
7	$85\% \rightarrow 12\,500$ $100\% \rightarrow 12\,500 \times \dfrac{100}{85}$ $= 14\,705$ $= £14\,700$ (nearest £100)	✔ ✔ ✔ ✔	 4	Set up 'proportion'. Set up calculation. Perform calculation. Round correctly.	This is a typical 'reverse percentage' question.	See Chapter 1

Question	Working	Mark		Note	Hint	HTP
8 a)	mean = 51p $$\sum(x-\bar{x})^2 = 84$$ $$\text{s.d.} = \sqrt{\frac{84}{6-1}} = 4\cdot1\text{p}$$	✔ ✔ ✔		Find the mean. Find total of $(x-\bar{x})^2$. Substitute into formula.	In your comparisons you must refer to the prices. Do not say, for example, 'the mean is lower' or similar.	See Chapter 18
b)	On average supermarkets were cheaper and more consistently priced.	✔ ✔	5	Include 'on average'. Refer to both mean and standard deviation.		
9	Use area of triangle formula. $$A = \tfrac{1}{2}bc\sin A$$ $$= \tfrac{1}{2}(30)(30)\sin 110$$ $$= 422\cdot86 \ (\times 2)$$ $$= 845\cdot7 \text{ cm}^2$$	✔ ✔ ✔ ✔	4	Clearly state formula. Substitute values. Calculate area of triangle. Know to double.	Look for use of area formula in questions such as these. State formula, then substitute.	See Chapter 16
10 a)	$a = 3$ because $\tfrac{1}{2}$ distance from 'top to trough' is 3. $b = 1$ because graph is then moved up 1 unit.	✔ ✔		One mark for each statement.	Make sure you know how to interpret graphs like this.	See Chapter 17
b)	$3\sin x + 1 = 3$ $3\sin x = 2$ $$\sin x = \frac{2}{3}$$ $x = \sin^{-1}\frac{2}{3} = 41\cdot8$ $180 - 41\cdot8 = 138\cdot2$ A is at $x = 41\cdot8$ B is at $x = 138\cdot2$	✔ ✔ ✔ ✔	6	Set up equation. Rearrange to make $\sin x$ the subject. Find x-value for A. Find x-value for B.	Use the CAST diagram to determine two quadrants for solutions.	
11 a)	Area of sector $$= \frac{35}{360} \times \pi \times 1\cdot25^2 = 0\cdot48 \text{ m}^2$$	✔ ✔		Substitute into formula, using correct radius and angle. Calculate solution.	In arc and sector questions, check carefully that you have used the correct angle AND the correct radius/diameter.	See Chapter 12
b)	$$\text{Arc} = \frac{35}{360} \times \pi \times 2 \times 25$$ $$= 15\cdot3 \text{ m}$$	✔ ✔ ✔	6	Substitute into formula, using correct diameter. Calculate solution.		

Question	Working	Mark		Note	Hint	HTP
12	Use Pythagoras' Theorem. $90^2 + 60^2$ $= 11\,700$ $110^2 = 12\,100$ $90^2 + 60^2 \neq 110^2$ ∴ by converse of Pythagoras' Theorem it is NOT a right-angled triangle.	✔ ✔ ✔	3	1 mark for calculating $90^2 + 60^2$. 1 mark for comparing with 110^2. 1 mark for conclusion.	Note when using converse of Pythagoras do not start by saying $90^2 + 60^2 = 110^2$ then working out. Take each 'section', then compare.	See Chapter 10
13 a) b)	 $230 - 180 = 50$ $110 - 50 = 60$ Angle LFS = 60° Alternative strategy: Identify co-interior angle on diagram. Calculate LFS $(360 - 70 - 230 = 60)$. $f^2 = l^2 + s^2 - 2ls \cos F$ $\quad = 16^2 + 42^2 - 2(16)(42)\cos 60$ $\quad = 1348$ $f = 36\cdot7\,\text{km}$	 ✔ ✔ (✔) (✔) ✔ ✔ ✔	5	Draw diagram and mark in 'Z' angle (110°). Determine 50° from 230° – 180°. Angle LFS = 110 – 50. Use the cosine rule. Substitute in F, l and s. Find length F.	You should recognise this as a sine/cosine rule question.	See Chapter 16

Practice Paper B

Paper 1 (non-calculator)

Question	Working	Mark		Note	Hint	HTP
1	$\dfrac{5}{3}+\dfrac{4}{7}$ $=\dfrac{(35+12)}{21}$ $=\dfrac{47}{21}=2\dfrac{5}{21}$	✔ ✔	2	Write mixed number as improper fraction. Correct denominator. Solution.		See Chapter 1
2	$25a^2-9b^2$ $(5a)^2-(3b)^2$ $(5a-3b)(5a+3b)$	✔ ✔	2	Write as difference of two squares and factorise fully.	When factorising check: ■ common factor ■ difference of two squares ■ trinomial/ quadratic.	See Chapter 2
3	$125^{\frac{2}{3}}$ $=5^2$ $=25$	✔ ✔	2	Take cube root. Square.	When working with fractional powers, it is usually easier to do the root first, then the power.	See Chapter 3
4	$m^{\frac{1}{2}+\frac{1}{2}}-m^{\frac{1}{2}+-\frac{1}{2}}$ $=m-1$	✔ ✔	2	Apply the laws of indices. Simplify.	Make sure you know the laws of indices, e.g. $m^0=1$	See Chapter 3
5	$AB^2=\left(\sqrt{20}\right)^2+\left(\sqrt{30}\right)^2$ $=20+30$ $=50$ $AB=\sqrt{50}$ $=5\sqrt{2}$	✔ ✔ ✔	3	Use Pythagoras' Theorem. Simplify the surd.	$\sqrt{50}=\sqrt{25}\times\sqrt{2}$ $=5\sqrt{2}$	See Chapters 3 and 10
6	$k=\sqrt{\dfrac{a}{b}}$ $k^2=\dfrac{a}{b}$ $bk^2=a$	 ✔ ✔	2	 Square both sides. Multiply by the denominator.		See Chapter 5

B

Question	Working	Mark		Note	Hint	HTP
7	$A = \pi r^2$ $\dfrac{16}{\pi} = \pi r^2$ $16 = \pi^2 r^2$ $\dfrac{4}{\pi} = r$ $C = 2\pi r$ $\quad = 2\pi \dfrac{4}{\pi}$ $\quad = 8$	✔ ✔ ✔ ✔	4	Use area formula to find r. Substitute for r in circumference formula.		See Chapter 12
8	$f(x) = 5 - x^2$ $f(-3) = 5 - (-3)^2$ $\quad\quad = -4$	✔ ✔	2	Correct substitution for x. Solution.	You should recognise function notation and know how to find a value.	See Chapter 6
9	$\dfrac{1}{x} + \dfrac{2}{x-1}$ $= \dfrac{x-1+2x}{x(x-1)}$ $= \dfrac{3x-1}{x(x-1)}$	✔ ✔ ✔	3	State common denominator. Correct numerator. Simplify.		See Chapter 4
10	Area $= \frac{1}{2} bc\sin A$ $= \frac{1}{2} \times AC \times 6 \times 0.75$ $18 = \frac{1}{2} \times AC \times 6 \times 0.75$ $2.25 \times AC = 18$ $AC = 18 \div 2.25$ $= 8\,cm$	✔ ✔ ✔ ✔	4	Substitute into area formula. Form equation. Rearrange to AC =. Solution.	Area of a triangle using trigonometry. Write down formula. Substitute known values. Calculate unknown variable.	See Chapter 16
11 a)	$(3, -4)$	✔✔		Use $(x-a)^2 + b$.	This question assesses your knowledge of the quadratic graph and quadratic function.	See Chapters 2 and 8
b)	$(0, 5)$	✔		Substitute $x = 0$ into equation of curve.		
c)	$(x-3)^2 - 4 = 0$ $(x-3)^2 = 4$ $x - 3 = \pm 2$ $x = \pm 2 + 3$ $x = 1, x = 5$ B $(1, 0)$, D $(5, 0)$ $BD = 4$	✔ ✔ ✔	6	Substitute $y = 0$ into equation of curve. Rearrange. Find both values of x. Find co-ordinates of B and D. State length of BD.		

Question	Working	Mark		Note	Hint	HTP
12	$y = 2x - 3$; $x + 2y = 14$ $x + 2(2x - 3) = 14$ $5x = 20$ $x = 4$ $y = 2(4) - 3$ $y = 5$ P (4, 5)	✔ ✔ ✔ ✔	4	Substitute for y in second equation. Find first variable. Find second variable. State co-ordinates of P.	Note that the question states 'algebraically', so do not use a geometry approach.	See Chapter 7
13 a)	Perimeter $= (2x + 5 + x + 3) \times 2$ $= 6x + 16$	✔		(Length + breadth) × 2. Calculate perimeter.		See Chapter 5
b)	Perimeter square $= 4(3x + 1)$ $= 12x + 4$ $12x + 4 = 6x + 16$ $6x = 12$ $x = 2$	✔ ✔		Form equation. Solution.		
c)	Difference = area of square − area of rectangle $= 49 - 45$ $= 4\,cm^2$	✔	4	Solution.		

Paper 2

Question	Working	Mark		Note	Hint	HTP
1	$(5\cdot88 \times 10^{12}) \div (3\cdot15 \times 10^{7})$ $= 18\ 666\cdot66$ $= 1\cdot87 \times 10^{5}$	✔ ✔ ✔	**3**	Set up division. Divide. Answer in scientific notation to 3 significant figures.		See Chapter 3
2	$m = \dfrac{(1-4)}{(4+2)}$ $= -\dfrac{1}{2}$ $y - b = m(x - a)$ $y - 1 = -\dfrac{1}{2}(x - 4)$ $y = -\dfrac{1}{2}x + 3$	 ✔ ✔ ✔	 **3**	Calculate gradient. Substitute values into formula. Simplify.	Straight-line question, so you need the gradient and one point on the line.	See Chapter 6
3	$\text{Arc} = \dfrac{130}{360}$ of circumference $\text{Arc} = \dfrac{130}{360} \times \pi \times d$ $= \dfrac{130}{360} \times \pi \times 28$ Perimeter $=$ arc $+ 2 \times$ radii $= 31\cdot8 + 28$ $= 59\cdot8\,\text{cm}$	✔ ✔ ✔ ✔	 **4**	Correct fraction. Substitute into formula. Correct method. Solution.	This is a typical arc question. Look carefully at the wording – here you need to find the perimeter, not just the length of the arc.	See Chapter 12
4	$= \dfrac{\sin^2 x}{\cos^2 x}$ $= \left(\dfrac{\sin x}{\cos x}\right)^2$ $= \tan^2 x$	✔ ✔	 **2**	Identify $1 - \sin^2 x = \cos^2 x$. Identify $\dfrac{\sin x}{\cos x} = \tan x$.	There are two identities you need to know: $\sin^2 x + \cos^2 x = 1$ and $\dfrac{\sin x}{\cos x} = \tan x$.	See Chapter 17
5	$2x^2 - 3x - 7 = 0$ $a = 2, b = -3, c = -7$ $x = \dfrac{-b \pm \sqrt{b^2 - 4ac}}{2a}$ $x = \dfrac{3 \pm \sqrt{(-3)^2 - 4(2)(-7)}}{2(2)}$ $x = \dfrac{3 + \sqrt{65}}{4}$ or $\dfrac{3 - \sqrt{65}}{4}$ $x = 2\cdot766$ or $-1\cdot266$ $x = 2\cdot8$ or $-1\cdot3$ (to 2 s.f.)	 ✔ ✔ ✔ ✔	 **4**	Substitute into formula. Evaluate $b^2 - 4ac$. Unrounded roots. Rounded roots.	The wording 'give *your* answer to 2 significant figures' implies the equation will not factorise easily so *you* need to use the formula. Remember to write *your* unrounded answers, and then round.	See Chapter 9

Question	Working	Mark		Note	Hint	HTP
6 a)	Median 32·5 Q1 = 14, Q3 = 46 $\text{SIQR} = \left(\dfrac{46-14}{2}\right) = 16$	✔ ✔ ✔		Median. Q1 and Q3. Semi-interquartile range. Valid comment regarding median.	To find median and quartiles, remember to write the list in order.	See Chapter 18
b)	The second group's marks were lower on average and they were more varied.	✔ ✔	5	Valid comment regarding semi-interquartile range.		
7	Volume of water = vol. big cone – vol. small cone. $V = \left(\frac{1}{3} \times \pi \times R^2 \times H\right)$ $\quad - \left(\frac{1}{3} \times \pi \times r^2 \times h\right)$ $= \left(\frac{1}{3} \times \pi \times 15^2 \times 22\right)$ $\quad - \left(\frac{1}{3} \times \pi \times 4^2 \times 8\right)$ $= 5181 - 133{\cdot}97$ $= 5047{\cdot}03$ $= 5000\,\text{cm}^3$ to 2 significant figures.	✔ ✔ ✔ ✔ ✔	 5	Strategy. Correct set-up of formula. Substitution of correct radii and heights. Unrounded solution. Rounded to 2 significant figures.	In these volume questions – look carefully at the diagram. Check you are using correct radius and height measurements.	See Chapter 14
8	$\cos x = \dfrac{12^2 + 10^2 - 5^2}{2(12)(10)}$ $\cos x = \dfrac{219}{240}$ $x = 24{\cdot}1°$	✔ ✔ ✔	 3	Substitute into cosine rule. Evaluate. Find angle. (Acute angle only is required.)	This is a typical sine/cosine rule question. Look at the information given and use the correct rule. Check what degree of accuracy is required.	See Chapter 16
9	Linear scale factor $= \dfrac{125}{90}$ Area scale factor $= \left(\dfrac{125}{90}\right)^2$ $\qquad = 1{\cdot}93$ No it is not double the area, as $1{\cdot}93 < 2$.	✔ ✔ ✔ ✔	 4	State linear scale factor. Square to get area scale factor. Area scale factor. Communicate solution.	Scale factor questions will normally involve area or volume – so check you know which scale factor to use.	See Chapter 13

Question	Working	Mark		Note	Hint	HTP
10	$3\sin x + 2 = 0$ $\sin x = \frac{-2}{3}$ (angle in quad 3 and 4) Acute angle $= 41\cdot8°$ $x = 180 + 41\cdot8,\ 360 - 41\cdot8$ $\quad = 221\cdot8,\ 318\cdot2$	✔ ✔ ✔ **3**		Rearrange to $\sin x$. Find acute angle. Find solutions.	Simple trigonometry equation type question. Remember to use 'CAST' diagram to determine quadrants.	See Chapter 17
11	$\mathbf{u} = \begin{pmatrix} 2 \\ -4 \end{pmatrix} \quad \mathbf{v} = \begin{pmatrix} -1 \\ 2 \end{pmatrix}$ $\mathbf{u} + \mathbf{v} = \begin{pmatrix} 1 \\ -2 \end{pmatrix}$	✔ ✔ **2**		Components of **u** and **v**. Solution.	Either write components or sketch vectors 'head to toe'.	See Chapter 15
12	$\begin{array}{ccc} \% & & £ \\ 120 & \to & 360 \\ 100 & \to & 360 \times \frac{100}{120} \\ & & = £300 \end{array}$	✔ ✔✔ **3**		Evidence of 120% $= 360$. Correct method. State answer.	This is a typical 'reverse percentage' calculation. Check if it involves increase or decrease. Always $\times$ by $\frac{100}{\%\text{age}}$.	See Chapter 1
13	 $\dfrac{AT}{\sin 35} = \dfrac{400}{\sin 100}$ $AT = \dfrac{400 \sin 35}{\sin 100}$ $\quad = 233\,\text{m}$	✔ ✔ ✔ ✔ ✔ **5**		Complete angles on diagram (45°, 35°, 100°). Substitute values into the sine rule. Rearrange. Calculate solution.	This is a typical sine/cosine rule question.	See Chapter 16
14	$60 - 25 = 35\,\text{cm}$ $x^2 = 60^2 - 35^2$ $\quad = 2375$ $x = 48\cdot7$ Width $AB = 48\cdot7 \times 2$ $\quad\quad = 97\cdot4\,\text{cm}$	✔ ✔ ✔ ✔ **4**		Identify triangle with base $\frac{1}{2}$ of AB, hypotenuse $\frac{1}{2}$ of 120 cm; find height. Use Pythagoras' Theorem to find base of triangle. Perform calculation. Multiply by 2 to find width.	This is a typical 'Pythagoras in a circle' question. 	See Chapter 12

Practice Paper C

Paper 1 (non-calculator)

Question	Working	Mark	Note	Hint	HTP
1	$\dfrac{3}{4}$ of $3\dfrac{1}{2} - 1\dfrac{5}{8}$ $\dfrac{3}{4} \times \dfrac{7}{2} = \dfrac{21}{8}$ $\dfrac{21}{8} - \dfrac{13}{8}$ $= \dfrac{8}{8}$ $= 1$	✔ ✔ ✔ **3**	Correct order of operations. Multiply, then subtract. Answer in simplest form.		See Chapter 1
2	$m = \dfrac{5t + t}{3 - 1}$ $= \dfrac{6t}{2}$ $= 3t$	✔ ✔ **2**	Use gradient formula.	$m = \dfrac{y_2 - y_1}{x_2 - x_1}$	See Chapter 6
3	$3x(x^2 - 2x + 5) + 4(x^2 - 2x + 5)$ $= 3x^3 - 6x^2 + 15x + 4x^2 - 8x + 20$ $= 3x^3 - 2x^2 + 7x + 20$	✔ ✔ ✔ **3**	Any three terms correct. Other three terms correct. Collect like terms.		See Chapter 2
4	$2x^2 - 5x - 3 = 0$ $(2x + 1)(x - 3) = 0$ $x = -\dfrac{1}{2}, x = 3$	 ✔ ✔✔ **3**		The ability to factorise a trinomial is a core skill.	See Chapter 9
5	$\sqrt{125} - 4\sqrt{5}$ $= \sqrt{(25 \times 5)} - 4\sqrt{5}$ $= 5\sqrt{5} - 4\sqrt{5}$ $= \sqrt{5}$	✔ ✔ **2**	Split surd. Simplify.	When simplifying a surd, look for perfect squares.	See Chapter 3
6	$\overrightarrow{BD} = \overrightarrow{BG} + \overrightarrow{GC} + \overrightarrow{CD}$ $= \mathbf{q} + \mathbf{p} + \mathbf{q}$ $= \mathbf{p} + 2\mathbf{q}$	✔ ✔ **2**	Find suitable path. Look for equivalent vectors. State vector pathway.		See Chapter 15
7	$x^{\frac{8}{5}} + 5x^0$ $= x^{\frac{8}{5}} + 5$	✔ ✔ **2**	Apply the laws of indices. Deal with x^0.	Learn all the laws of indices and recognise which one to use.	See Chapter 3

Question	Working	Mark		Note	Hint	HTP
8 a)	$x^2 - 2x - 15$ $= (x-5)(x+3)$ $a = 3, b = -5$	✔ ✔		Factorising correctly. Correct values allocated to a and b.		See Chapter 8
b)	Roots are $x = -3$ and $x = 5$	✔		Correct roots.		
c)	Mid-point of roots $= 1$ $y = 1^2 - 2(1) - 15$ $= -16$ Turning point$(1, -16)$	✔ ✔ ✔	6	Mid-point of -3 to 5. Substitute into equation of curve. State turning point.		
9	Let t = T/F questions and m = multiple choice questions. $t + m = 20$ $3t + 11m = 100$ $3t + 3m = 60$ $8m = 40$ $m = 5$ $t + 5 = 20$ $t = 15$ Number of T/F questions is 15. Number of multiple choice questions is 5.	✔ ✔ ✔ ✔ ✔ ✔	6	Form first equation. Form second equation. Scale up. Find value of first variable. Find value of second variable. Solution.	This is typical wording for a simultaneous equations question. Check if question asks for values of variables – or for another calculation.	See Chapter 7
10	$V = \frac{4}{3}\pi r^3$ $\frac{3V}{4} = \pi r^3$ $\frac{3V}{4\pi} = r^3$ $r = \sqrt[3]{\frac{3V}{4\pi}}$	✔ ✔ ✔	3	$\div \frac{4}{3}\left(\text{or} \times \frac{3}{4}\right)$ $\div \pi$ Cube root.	When dealing with changing the subject, do one step at a time and write each line down clearly.	See Chapter 14
11	$AB^2 = 2^2 - (2\sin x)^2$ $= 4 - 4\sin^2 x$ $= 4(1 - \sin^2 x)$ $= 4\cos^2 x$ $AB = \sqrt{4\cos^2 x}$ $= 2\cos x$	✔ ✔ ✔	3	Use Pythagoras' Theorem. Use the identity $\sin^2 x + \cos^2 x = 1$.	In a right-angled triangle consider using Pythagoras' Theorem. Then consider trigonometry identifies.	See Chapters 10 and 17

Question	Working	Mark		Note	Hint	HTP
12 a)	$\dfrac{b(b+2)}{5(b+2)}$	✔✔		Factorise top and bottom.		See Chapter 2
	$=\dfrac{b}{5}$	✔		Cancel $b+2$.		
b)	$6xy^2 - 15x^3y$	✔		Finding common factor.		
	$3xy(2y - 5x^2)$	✔	5	Complete factorising.		

Paper 2

Question	Working	Mark		Note	Hint	HTP
1	$\begin{array}{cc}\% & \pounds \\ 103 \to 16\,995\end{array}$ $100 \to 16\,995 \times \dfrac{100}{103}$ $= \pounds16\,500$	✔ ✔ ✔	 3	Evidence of 103% = 16 995. Correct method. Solution.	This is a typical 'reverse percentage' calculation. Are you expecting a bigger or smaller answer? Always multiply by $\dfrac{100}{\%\,\text{age}}$.	See Chapter 1
2	$(x+1)^2 - 1 - 1$ $(x+1)^2 - 2$	✔ ✔	 2	Halve the coefficient of x and complete the square. Write in the form $(x+p)^2 + q$.		See Chapter 2
3	Angle OTR = 90 Angle POT $\quad = 180 - 2 \times 36$ $\quad = 108$ Angle TOR = 72 $x = 180 - 90 - 72$ $\quad = 18$	✔ ✔ ✔	 3	Know radius and tangent meet at right angle. Calculate angle TOR. State value of x.		See Chapter 12
4	$f(x) = 2x + 3$ $f(-4) = 2(-4) + 3 = -5$ $b = -5$ $f(x) = 2x + 3$ $11 = 2x + 3$ $x = 4$ $a = 4$	 ✔ ✔ ✔	 3	Substitute –4 for x. State value of b. Substitute 11 for $f(x)$. State value of a.		See Chapter 6
5 a) b)	$a = $ amplitude $= 3$ $b = 1$(graph moved up 1 square) $3\cos x + 1 = 0$ $\cos x = \dfrac{-1}{3}$ (2nd and 3rd quadrants) Acute angle = 70·5 $x = 180 - 70\cdot5,$ $\quad 180 + 70\cdot5$ $\quad = 109\cdot5, 250\cdot5$	✔ ✔ ✔ ✔ ✔ ✔	 6	Amplitude $\frac{1}{2}$ 'top to trough'. Set $y = 0$ and form equation. Rearrange to get $\cos x$. Find first angle. Find second angle.	Difference from –2 to 4 is 6. Therefore amplitude is half of 6. Remember to use CAST diagram to determine quadrant. Question only asks for x co-ordinates.	See Chapter 17

Question	Working	Mark		Note	Hint	HTP
6 a)	$m = \dfrac{21-6}{2-7} = -3$ $y - b = m(x - a)$ $y - 21 = -3(x - 2)$	✔ ✔		Find the gradient. Use general equation of a straight line. Substitute gradient and one point in general equation of straight line.		See Chapter 18
	$y = -3x + 27$	✔		Write in terms of x and y.		
	$V = -3A + 27$			Write in context of V and A.		
b)	$V = -3A + 27$ $V = -3(8) + 27 = 3$ Value = £3000	✔ ✔	5	 Substitute into formula. Calculate value.		
7	Angle = 70°	✔		Find angle between first two legs.	This is a typical sine/cosine rule question.	See Chapter 16
	$a^2 = b^2 + c^2 - 2bc\cos A$ $= 300^2 + 550^2 - 2(300)$ $(550)\cos 70$ $= 279\,633$ $a = 529\,\text{km}$	✔ ✔ ✔	 4	 Substitute values into cosine rule. Evaluate a^2. Evaluate a.	Use parallel lines cut by transversal to calculate 70° or use co-interior angles.	
8	$V = \frac{1}{3}\pi r^2 h$ $125 = \frac{1}{3}\pi\, r^2\, 10$ $r^2 = \dfrac{125 \times 3}{10\pi}$ $r = \sqrt{\dfrac{125 \times 3}{10\pi}}$ $= 3\cdot454$ $d = 6\cdot91$	✔ ✔ ✔ ✔	 4	Substitute into volume formula. Form equation. Calculate r^2. Calculate diameter.	In volume questions; ensure you use correct radius and diameter.	See Chapter 14
9	$SF = \dfrac{8}{12} = \dfrac{2}{3}$ $AC = \dfrac{2}{3} \times 21$ $= 14\,\text{cm}$	✔✔ ✔	 3	Recognise similar triangles and calculate scale factor. State length of AC.	Make sure you can identify similar triangles in diagrams like this one.	See Chapter 13

Question	Working	Mark		Note	Hint	HTP
10 a)	$\sin x = \frac{1}{2}$ (angle in first and second quadrants)	✔		Rearrange equation to $\sin x =$.		See Chapter 17
	$x = 30$	✔		Find solution in first quadrant.		
	$x = 150$	✔		Find second solution.		
b)	$\frac{1}{3}x = 30, 150$					
	$x = 90, 450$	✔		Equate to previous solutions and calculate x value.		
	So $x = 90$	✔	**5**	Discard 450 (out of range).		
11 a)	mean $= \frac{385}{7} = 55\,\text{kg}$	✔		Calculate the mean.		See Chapter 18
b)	$(x-\bar{x})^2$ 169, 9, 4, 49, 49, 16, 256	✔		Calculate $\sum (x - \bar{x})^2$.		
	$\sum\left(x-\bar{x}\right)^2 = 552$					
	s.d. $= \sqrt{\dfrac{552}{6}}$	✔		Substitute into formula.		
	$= 9{\cdot}6\,\text{kg}$	✔		Calculate standard deviation.		
c)	On average the group of seven were lighter than whole year group but the whole year group weights were more consistent.	✔✔	**6**	Valid comment regarding mean. Valid comment regarding standard deviation.		
12	106 and **31**	✔		Calculate the missing angle(s) in the outer triangle.	This is a common style of question which mixes non-right-angled trigonometry with right-angled trigonometry (or sometimes Pythagoras' Theorem).	See Chapter 16
	$\dfrac{a}{\sin 43} = \dfrac{10}{\sin 31}$	✔		Substitute into sine rule.		
	$a = \dfrac{10\sin 43}{\sin 31}$	✔		Rearrange to $a =$.		
	$= 13{\cdot}2$	✔		Calculate a.		
	$\sin 74 = \dfrac{\text{height}}{13{\cdot}2}$					
	$H = 13{\cdot}2 \sin 74$	✔		Substitute value of a to $\sin = \dfrac{\text{opp}}{\text{hyp}}$.		
	Height $= 12{\cdot}7$ metres	✔	**6**	Calculate height.		